Original title:
Can Someone Just Tell Me the Point Already?

Copyright © 2025 Creative Arts Management OÜ
All rights reserved.

Author: Natalia Harrington
ISBN HARDBACK: 978-1-80566-032-3
ISBN PAPERBACK: 978-1-80566-327-0

Where's the Heart of This Matter?

In a sea of words I float,
Searching for some kind of note.
Questions swirl, like leaves in fall,
Where's the heart? I can't recall.

Each answer dances, swift and sly,
I raise my hand; oh, my oh my!
Can we skip the fluff and haze?
Just give me facts, save me the maze!

The Search for Substance

What's the deal with all this fluff?
I'm hungry now; I've had enough!
Words that twist, turn, and parade,
   Leave me lost in this charade.

I sift through tales and grand displays,
   Like a kid at a buffet craze.
Where's the meat? Where's the cheese?
Life feels like an endless tease!

In Pursuit of Meaning

I'm on a quest, a daring chase,
To find the meaning, face to face.
Left and right, I spin and twirl,
Like a cat lost in a whirl.

This riddle's dense; it plays all night,
With twists and turns that just feel tight.
If only clarity would come,
Or maybe bring a little fun!

Cut to the Chase

Let's skip the chatter, get to fries,
No need for fancy, no weird ties.
I want the straight, the raw, the bold,
Lost in stories, I've turned cold.

Break down the walls, cut all the fluff,
Time is ticking; it's more than tough.
Just give me truth in simple form,
Or I might just, well, lose my charm!

Hidden in Plain Sight

Where is the treasure, they say,
Hiding like socks in disarray.
Each clue leads us astray,
Puzzles dance and play.

Maps lead to nowhere, what a tease,
While I search through pots and trees.
The X marks the spot, oh please,
Just point me to the keys!

An Invitation to Understanding

Join me for coffee or tea,
While we ponder life's big mystery.
Conversations drift like a bee,
Where's the point? Now it's fuzzy.

Frothy cups, ideas collide,
As logic takes a rollercoaster ride.
With laughter, we both confide,
But clarity, we've denied.

The Frustration of Unfinished Thoughts

Ideas bubble up like stew,
Then vanish like morning dew.
You start, then lose the clue,
Leaving everyone askew.

Words hang heavy in the air,
Thoughts race but go nowhere.
The silence grips with flair,
Wondering if someone cares.

Tracing the Tangible

Trying to catch a fleeting line,
Like chasing shadows in sunshine.
Just trying to redraw the design,
While folks laugh at my decline.

I reach but grasp the void,
Questions swirling, none enjoyed.
Is the answer just avoided?
A riddle I've deployed!

Drowning in Ambiguity

Got my head above the water, yet here I stand,
Wading through the fog, can't understand.
Questions floating by, like leaves in a stream,
Where's the map for this wild, ridiculous dream?

Words twisting and twirling, like dancers at night,
Searching for the truth, but it's quite out of sight.
Laughing at my plight, it's a glorious mess,
Who knew confusion could wear such a dress?

The Endless Equation

There's an X and a Y, oh what could they mean?
Solving them feels like a bad movie scene.
The numbers keep piling like laundry to fold,
Endless digits marching, so distant and cold.

Papers all scattered, equations gone wild,
Staring at the screen like an abandoned child.
Just one simple answer, that's all that I crave,
Yet here I am, hopeless, like a lost little wave.

A Puzzle with Missing Pieces

Jigsaw pieces scattered, where did they go?
The corner of sanity? Well, it's just a no-show.
Trying to fit them, but they laugh in my face,
This game of confoundment? I've lost all my grace.

Colors don't match up, am I seeing it right?
The cat seems to know, but it's keeping it tight.
Chasing my tail like it's some kind of treat,
This puzzle gets funnier with every defeat.

Is It Just Me?

In a room full of chatter, I'm losing my track,
Thoughts bouncing 'round like a wild acrobat.
Everyone's nodding, but I'm in a daze,
Is this a conference, or am I just amazed?

Questions in circles, like a dog on a chase,
Witty remarks flying, oh, what a strange place.
While the crowd finds gold, I'm stuck at the gate,
Laughing at myself, well, isn't that fate?

Seeking Clarity in the Chaos

In a world full of chatter, loud and bold,
They're tossing coins, where's the gold?
I asked the owl, wise and serene,
He blinked and said, 'What does it mean?'

Questions float like balloons in the sky,
While answers sip tea, oh so spry.
I juggled my thoughts, dropped a few,
Is clarity hiding or just playing peek-a-boo?

The cat on the fence, with a knowing smile,
Said, 'Keep asking, it's worth your while.'
Yet here I am, lost in my quest,
For simple truths, I must invest.

So with every riddle and twist of fate,
I'll chuckle aloud, negotiate my state.
For deep in the mud, a gem might gleam,
If only I wake from this riddle-dream.

Answers Whispered in the Wind

The wind swirls and giggles, so carefree,
It carries secrets, one-two-three.
I lean in closer, trying to hear,
But all I get is a loud, 'Oh dear!'

In the trees, the leaves start to sway,
They dance around, then drift away.
Is there wisdom in the rustling sound?
Or just a squirrel, racing around?

A cloud floats by, with a cheeky grin,
'It's all nonsense,' it whispers in.
Yet still I wander, searching for clues,
In the abstract world of poetic blues.

So, I follow the breeze, with playful steps,
Hoping to dodge the vague missteps.
'Cos maybe the laughs hide truths so grand,
If one just lets go and takes a stand.

The Silence Between the Lines

Words dance on paper, but do they say?
Between the pauses, there's a fray.
An awkward silence, thick as glue,
What's left unsaid? A mystery too!

I read between lines, a comic book's flare,
Finding punchlines lost in thin air.
Each stanza's a jigsaw, parts of a whole,
But one piece is missing, where did it roll?

So I laugh at the riddles, take them in stride,
Through the labyrinth where puns abide.
A wink from the poet, a nudge from the text,
What's written is fluffed, and what's blank perplexed.

I sip my coffee, pondering this dance,
Do I take the leap or wait for a chance?
For in every chuckle, there's wisdom, I swear,
If only one could trace what's not spoken there.

Why Are We Still Waiting?

In a line that stretches, oh so long,
I hum to the tune of a silly song.
As time tick-tocks like a clock gone mad,
Why the delay? This waiting's a fad!

The queue is a circus, clowns on parade,
With stories piled high, and jokes well played.
I'm counting the seconds, one, two, three,
What's all the fuss? Just let it be!

An old man whispers, 'Patience, my friend,'
But my laughter is loud, it starts to offend.
A cat runs by, carrying dreams,
In a world that giggles, or so it seems.

So here I wait, with giggles and gleams,
In the echoing laughter of whimsical themes.
Is there meaning, divine in delay?
Or just a punchline that's come out to play?

Lost in Translation

Words dance on tongues, yet meanings stray,
Lost in the chatter, we stumble and play.
Like jesters in court, we jest and we laugh,
Missing the message, we just chase the gaff.

Conversations swirl, like leaves in a breeze,
Hints of the meaning slip past with such ease.
Finding the focus, a wild goose chase,
We twirl and we tangle, it's all a big race.

The Fable of Discontent

Sitting in circles, we ponder and frown,
Chasing the tales that keep dragging us down.
The moral is muddled, the plot's out of sync,
We're waiting for wisdom, but all that we think.

Once upon a time, the rabbit asked why,
He chased after answers, but let out a sigh.
For every bright promise was wrapped in a joke,
And every response just a puff of cold smoke.

Signposts of the Soul

Guiding our hearts, the signposts are bent,
Each arrow points nowhere, oh what a mess!
We search for the truth, like kids on a quest,
Do we follow the path, or just guess like the rest?

With every direction, we lose a few screws,
Is left really left, or just more of the blues?
The signs flash their riddles, but none seem quite clear,
Yet still we keep laughing, pretending we steer.

Unanswered Yearnings

In the land of desire, we stake out our claims,
But answers grow legs, and they run with our games.
What's the point of wishing if wishes just fade,
A circus of thought, where fun plans invade?

Every "what if" leads to a chuckle or two,
We ponder our dreams while we search for the clue.
The questions keep piling, like shoes by the door,
Yet maybe the joy's in the hunt, evermore.

Answers Yielding Frustration

I asked a thousand questions,
Responses in a jumbled mess.
A maze of words, oh what a thrill,
Yet here I am, still seeking still.

Thought I'd find the light today,
But it feels like a game we play.
Dancing round ideas that stall,
This endless loop, a comedic brawl.

The Weight of the Unsaid

Beneath the smiles, an awkward pause,
Words hang like laundry without cause.
We laugh and chat, yet deep down know,
The answers hide, just for show.

Why speak the truth when we can jest?
In riddles and rhymes, we find unrest.
The unasked question spins and twirls,
As logic fights with silly swirls.

The Allure of the Obvious

Oh, the obvious sits right there,
Like a cat with its smug little stare.
We stroll around it, oh what a quest,
A grand parade for a simple jest.

Why make it hard, or build a wall?
When clarity can be a simple call?
Yet here we sit, so blissfully lost,
Chasing lines, counting the cost.

Shadows of Insight

In shadows, wisdom plays a game,
Flickers of thought that never claim.
Laughter echoes, lost in the fade,
As logic bids us, "I'm afraid."

We seek the truth in riddled rain,
Yet find ourselves, quite insane.
With every insight that we seek,
Why does the answer take a peek?

Puzzle Pieces That Don't Fit

In a box full of pieces, I sit and I sigh,
Searching for answers, but they all just fly by.
The edge ones are great, but the middle ones tease,
Like socks in the dryer, they just don't appease.

I flip and I turn, trying hard to align,
But they jigsaw around, not a hint of a sign.
A dog chews my corner, my coffee's gone cold,
Yet I press on with zeal, for the tale to unfold.

The Search for Substance

A sandwich so scrumptious, yet hollow within,
Bite after bite, where's the tasty win?
I search for a flavor, something to savor,
But all I discover is intricate behavior.

Like jokes without punchlines, they leave me bemused,\nEach line that I follow feels oddly confused.
I laugh with a shrug, at my quest in the void,
In a world full of fluff, my patience it's toyed.

Threads of Confusion

A tapestry woven with colors so bright,
Yet the patterns don't match, and they give me a fright.
Are they flowers or creatures, or hats that we wear?
This jumble of nonsense gives me quite a scare.

I tug one loose thread, and the whole thing unspools,
Chaos erupts, like a class full of fools.
"Is this art?" I ponder, with a laugh and a grin,
As I wrap up my thoughts in this whirlwind of spin.

The Wanderer's Riddle

On a quest for the meaning, I wander so far,
Through valleys of nonsense and gardens bizarre.
Each signpost I find leads me further astray,
Is it north, south, or just a game that you play?

With a map filled with riddles and clues that confound,
I chuckle aloud, as I spin round and round.
For the journey's the joke, and the punchline's a twist,
It's the laughter of life that I secretly missed.

Fragments of Revelation

Every day I ponder hard,
Yet answers seem to drift apart.
I ask the crowd, I check the cards,
Still none can share their art.

The coffee's cold, the toast is burnt,
Is wisdom hiding in the fridge?
The more I crave, the more I yearn,
For signs to cross that great big ridge.

A squirrel chases after a nut,
While I'm just chasing thoughts,
In riddles wrapped, in puzzles shut,
Oh, life, you've got me caught!

The clock ticks loud, it's late for work,
I wave goodbye to reason's chase.
If knowledge is a cheerful perk,
Why's it sprinting from my face?

The Gap Between Dreams and Knowing

In dreams, I'm soaring high and free,
But daylight brings a heavy frown.
What's real? Just coffee and a bee,
Buzzing 'round my sleepy town.

I skip the map, just take a chance,
My mind's a circus, wild and bright.
I hear the laughter, feel the dance,
But then I trip—oh what a sight!

"Just follow me," they all declare,
Yet everyone seems lost inside.
The answers float on puffy air,
While logic takes a sudden ride.

With dreams, I'm armed; with doubts, I'm bare,
Perhaps I'll learn to spin and twirl.
Life's joy is more than just a dare,
It's fun to watch the mystery unfurl!

Echoes of Uncertainty

I asked a shadow, got no speech,
Just silence wrapped around my shoe.
The wind has tales it cannot teach,
And what's a sage without a clue?

The trees are tweeting like alarmed,
While squirrels argue what's the plan.
I ponder if I'm simply charmed,
Or lost inside a daft old scan.

A feather floats on morning dew,
It whispers secrets, but I'm slow.
It's funny how I never knew,
The biggest laugh is just to go!

With every step, I'm tripping fate,
Collecting giggles on the way.
If life's a game, don't hesitate,
Just find the punchline and play!

Navigating the Unknown

On this wild ride, I hold the wheel,
But GPS is lost on me.
I turn left, right, can't help but feel,
The map is just a mystery.

A compass spins in dizzy dance,
While paper planes just mock my plight.
Perhaps it's time to take a chance,
And follow clouds that float in flight.

I think of all the signs I've seen,
From fortune cookies now in pieces.
Like jellybeans, my thoughts careen,
While sense of purpose just decreases.

Yet here I laugh and chase the stars,
With humor guiding every move.
The unknown's not so far from ours,
Just fun adventures to improve!

The Long Walk to Answers

In a maze of thoughts I roam,
Each turn leads me far from home.
Question marks dance in the air,
Why so many? It's not quite fair!

I ask a bird, it just goes tweet,
A squirrel laughs, this can't be sweet.
An old tree sighs, 'Ah, you'll see',
But what it means remains a mystery!

The path is twisty, full of quirks,
Where logic plays and reason lurks.
I trip on riddles, skip on clues,
Is there a map, or just a ruse?

With every step, a chuckle grows,
At this silly dance with life's woes.
So here I am, feet sore and gray,
Still wandering, come what may!

What Lies Ahead?

I peek around a corner tight,
Hoping to see clear daylight.
But shadows whisper, 'Not today',
Just more questions in disarray!

I strut and fret, a curious cat,
In search of wisdom, imagine that!
But signs are hazy, roads are long,
Turns out, no one knows a song.

A turtle grins, 'Chill out, friend',
While I just want this to end.
'What's next?' I shout, with playful glee,
He shrugs it off, 'Just let it be'.

So off I wander, with a frown,
In a world that spins upside down.
But laughter bubbles up like foam,
In this wacky quest that feels like home!

Unsung Melodies of Meaning

Each note I chase sounds out of tune,
Like cats on keys beneath the moon.
I hum a tune that leads to doubt,
What's the chorus? I can't figure out!

In the orchestra of daily grind,
The rhythm's lost, the beat unkind.
I shake my head, tap my shoe,
Waiting for someone to give a clue.

Is it a solo or group affair?
I'm lost in the notes of thin air.
While life plays on, a jazzy spree,
I just need a hint: What's the key?

But laughter bursts like a trumpet's blast,
In this chaotic symphony cast.
So I'll dance along, with humor spun,
Searching for meaning, but having fun!

Crack the Code of Clarity

In a room filled with chatter, the clock starts to spin,
Words dance in circles, I'm lost in the din.
Questions stack high like a tower of cheese,
I'm craving some insight, or at least some unease.

Hints wrapped in riddles, my brain starts to ache,
Is there a decoder for this puzzling quake?
Nods and winks fly like confetti in air,
But the meaning stays hidden, the truth's unaware.

Guides with their maps keep saying, 'Just wait!',
But the waiting's a game that I can't seem to sate.
I chuckle and giggle, though lost in the fray,
Maybe the fun's in the mess of the play.

So I'll sip on my coffee and let laughter flow,
In the circus of jargon, I'm the main show.
With a wink and a grin, I'll embrace this whole dance,
'Cause clarity's overrated—give chaos a chance!

A Journey Without a Map

They handed me directions, but they're all upside down,
Other travelers giggle, they're wearing a frown.
I set forth on foot, without so much as a clue,
Lost in the wonder, with nowhere to view.

Around every corner, confusion does swell,
Is this a detour, or have I arrived in hell?
The sun's feeling cheeky—it's a trickster, you see,
As I wander these paths where I'm meant to be free.

Voices are bubbling like soda, so bright,
"Just follow your heart," they cheer with delight.
But my heart's taking scenic routes—what a show,
While the end of this journey stays hidden, oh no!

With giggles and gaffes, I stroll and I sway,
The point of my travel? Just indulge in the play.
Maps are for losers who cannot embrace fun,
So here's to the journey—adventure's begun!

Beneath the Surface

Diving in deep, where the waters churn,
I'm hunting for meaning, but dreams take a turn.
Fish with strange faces swim past with a grin,
Elusive the answers, but let the games begin!

Bubbles of nonsense pop up all around,
Submerged in the jovial, no clarity found.
They laugh and they splash, oh what a mad show,
As I search for a beacon, but only find flow.

A treasure chest labeled "Forget what you knew,"
I unlock with a giggle, oh what do I rue?
The gold is just glitter, the diamonds are dreams,
And wisdom's a jester, or so it seems.

So I float with the current, my mind in a whirl,
The deeper I go, the more I could twirl.
In the depths of confusion, let humor thrive bright,
For beneath the dark waters, it's giggles I write!

What Lies Beneath?

Underneath the surface, there's laughter and jest,
What lies in the shadows is truly a quest.
Poking and prodding at mysteries so grand,
Is it wisdom I'm seeking, or just a soft hand?

The bumpy road whispers, 'Come follow my lead,'
While my brain does somersaults on this nonsense steed.
Silly little hedgehogs roll by and just smile,
As they tumble through questions that pile in a pile.

So I catch their strange giggles and hold them for dear,
Each chuckle a riddle that brings me more cheer.
The point's a mirage, a joke in disguise,
And I find that I'm laughing through all of my sighs.

So let's dance in the chaos, let's party down low,
For what lies beneath is the best kind of show.
With a twinkle and quirk, we'll embrace all the fun,
As the search for the point leads us back to square one!

Navigating the Fog

In a maze of thoughts, I roam,
Lost in a fog, far from home.
Questions swirl like autumn leaves,
What's the answer? Oh, who believes!

Maps of clarity are hard to find,
I ask the trees, they're so unkind.
With every turn, I scratch my head,
Did I just pass that same old shed?

With a compass that spins and spins,
I'm baffled by these crazy whims.
The signs are clear, but not to me,
Guess I'll just sip my herbal tea!

Maybe there's wisdom in thick smoke,
Or is it just a silly joke?
One day I'll see, by chance or fate,
For now, I'll just contemplate!

The Core of Confusion

Wrapped in riddles, I think aloud,
Get lost in the chaos, a buzzing crowd.
Why ask questions when nonsense reigns?
It's a circus in my brain, oh what pains!

The answers hide like shy little sprites,
In corners where no one never smites.
I'll knock on doors, but they won't budge,
Maybe silence is the real grudge!

Puzzles twist in every direction,
Logic takes a vacation, what a selection!
Am I the jester in this grand play?
Laughing off truths that sway away.

Can a hint emerge, even vague?
Or is it just another brain plague?
Tiptoe through this circus of thoughts,
Expecting clarity, but confusion's what caught!

Sifting Through Shadows

In dim lit corners, whispers creep,
Through tangled thoughts, the mind loses sleep.
Fumbling around, I search for a sign,
Where's the punchline or the divine?

The shadows dance, they twist and twirl,
In the fog of nonsense, I give a whirl.
Questions stack like laundry high,
When did life turn into this sly fly?

Shadows chuckle, they know the score,
While I just wonder, "Is there more?"
Hours pass, I'm stuck in this game,
Will the light switch on, or remain the same?

I sift through giggles and sighs,
Seeking sense in these whacky lies.
But finding clarity feels like a blink,
Maybe it's me, or maybe I stink!

The Silence Between Us

Amidst the noise, there's a comic pause,
As we dance around the truth that draws.
What's the point of this game we play?
Is there wisdom in what we don't say?

With every glance, a question soars,
Through awkward laughter and open doors.
Do we know the rules of this charade?
Or are we just actors with a bad trade?

Between conspiratorial whispers we tread,
Mapping out thoughts, yet feeling misled.
What's unspoken could fill a book,
Still, we chuckle and steal a look.

So here's to gaps and the silence they dress,
In each empty moment, don't stress!
Let's ride the waves of this endless jest,
Finding joy in what we could've expressed!

The Unfurling Mystery

A cat walks by with quite the flair,
With secrets swirling in the air.
I ask him why he struts around,
He just blinks once and looks profound.

The clouds all gather, skies turn grey,
The coffee's cold, but coffee's okay.
A fortune teller gives her take,
Yet all I hear is her rubber snake.

The clock ticks on, what's the plan?
Is fortune hiding in a can?
With riddles wrapped in cheese and yarn,
The answers dance, then slowly turn.

So here I sit, with crumbs and dreams,
Unraveling all these little schemes.
Perhaps the punchline's not so near,
Oh wait, it was just my dog's rear!

Wading Through the Muddled Waters

A fish swims by, it winks at me,
I ponder if it wants some tea.
With water swirling, what's the catch?
Is it highbrow way to meet a hatch?

My boots are soaked, I leap and splash,
Wading through muddle with a dash.
I chase the fish, it turns and mocks,
Where's all the wisdom in its socks?

A frog croaks loudly, flies take flight,
I wave goodbye to sense and sight.
In ripples deep, a riddle looms,
Is clarity hiding amidst the blooms?

So here I float in puzzlement,
With every gust, a new bent.
Oh, to be clear as pond's still glass,
Instead, I sip from waters vast!

Speaking in Riddles

A man in a hat speaks with flair,
His words are tangled, twist in air.
He tells of gold that's just a spin,
And how it all begins with "thin."

A riddle here, a riddle there,
I scratch my head, it's quite the affair.
He nods with glee, I get the sense,
His hidden jokes are ever dense.

By candlelight, the shadows dance,
Is he joking or just in a trance?
With every twist, my brain goes frazzled,
I'd trade this talk for a quick razzle.

Yet somehow I still find delight,
In all the twirls of this wild flight.
Perhaps the riddle's just for laughs,
While I'm still searching for the graphs.

The Yearning for Resolution

In the circus tent, a lion roars,
While jugglers balance on bikes and floors.
I ask the sage, "What's the end?"
He tosses up a coin, my friend.

A tightrope walker, sways and veers,
My heart beats fast, I fight my fears.
With every step, uncertainty reigns,
What is the point of all these chains?

The jester jests, "Life's a game!"
But I just want to know the name.
Confetti falls as I ponder deep,
Perhaps the truth's for now, not steep.

A fortune cookie waits for me,
"To find your way, just sip some tea."
So with a grin, I dare to toast,
To every riddle, I love the most!

The Eternal Inquiry

What's the deal with life's big quiz?
Every day it's a brand new whiz.
Questions piling, a never-end scroll,
Searching for answers, but where's the goal?

Maps and charts, I've got none in stock,
Tangled thoughts, like a knock-off clock.
Round and round, where's the exit sign?
Got the jitters, and feels like a crime!

I ask the wise, they smile and shrug,
Sipping their tea, giving a bug.
They chuckle, saying it's part of the game,
While I stand here, just feeling lame!

Is there a manual, a guide that I missed?
Or just stumble along, like a hopeful twist?
Answers are scarce like rain in the sun,
Laughing in circles, no end to the fun!

Veils of Confusion

I woke up today with stars in my eyes,
But all I can see are the world's silly lies.
Wrapped in questions like layers of cake,
Digging for meaning, how much will it take?

The wise ones chatter, but what do they mean?
They toss out phrases, acting all keen.
Like riddles and puzzles with missing pegs,
Frustration bubbles while my brain slowly begs!

I tried to decipher, but heads started spinning,
Should I laugh or cry? Where's the real winning?
Each thought is a maze, with no map in sight,
Wishing for clarity like it's a lost kite!

So here I am, caught up in the jest,
Navigating nonsense, doing my best.
Tell me, dear friend, if you've found the key,
To unlock all the laughter while I sip my tea!

Frustrations in the Fog

Fog rolls in, thick as a stew,
Questions pop up like a bad déjà vu.
I raise my hand, but it slips through the haze,
Wishing for sunlight to lighten my craze!

Every answer I seek is like a chase in the night,
Shadows of meaning just dart out of sight.
With each step I take, the path shifts anew,
Like a jigsaw puzzle with pieces askew!

Does anyone know if the point really glows?
Or am I just destined to ponder in throes?
Tick-tock goes the clock, with no end in view,
Laughter erupts as I try to break through!

So here I will wade, through the mist and the jive,
Swirling confusion, but still I feel alive.
Join in the fun, let's bask in the blur,
Finding joy in the questions, now that's the spur!

Voice of the Uninformed

Hey there, friend, I've got a big bone,
Sitting in wonder, feeling like a drone.
What's the magic trick to make it all clear?
Is it hidden in laughter or sipped with a beer?

The crowd shouts answers, a chorus of bees,
But goodness, their wisdom comes wrapped in a tease.
Each word spins around like a wacky old tune,
Dancing around logic, like it's a cartoon!

I scribble my notes, yet nothing makes sense,
Trying to decode this mixed-up suspense.
Do I follow the chatter or just trust my hunch?
Or maybe just snack and enjoy a nice munch?

So here's my cheer to the lost and the confused,
Just know that in laughter, we're all rather amused.
Let's join in the game, take a leap in the froth,
The answer is laughter, so let loose and troth!

Clarity in the Chaos

In a world where thoughts collide,
Questions bounce like balls of pride.
Why does the sun shine on my shoe?
What's the point? Who really knew?

Lost among the daily grind,
Searching for what's hard to find.
Charts and graphs, they spin and whirl,
While my mind just wants to twirl.

Cooked the pasta, but where's the sauce?
Is it worth the extra cross?
Life was simple, now it's tough,
And all the answers seem too rough.

So, let's laugh and take a stand,
Navigating this wacky land.
Grab a bowl of random fruit,
And munch on life's silly pursuit.

Echoes of Intention

Whispers float on evening air,
What's the reason, if you dare?
Hope it's not a game of charades,
With riddles wrapped in masquerades.

Clocks tick on, while I just sit,
Understanding seems to take a hit.
Was that a clue or just a jest?
My mind's a puzzle, not like the rest.

I asked the cat, he just meowed,
Feline wisdom tends not to shroud.
Chasing tails in circles spun,
Dig in deeper, oh what fun!

Will I find a treasure map?
Or just another silly trap?
Laughing loudly 'til I fall,
In echoes of it all, I call.

The Maze of Ambivalence

Round and round, a twisty fate,
Decisions large, yet I still wait.
What's behind that boxy door?
A sandwich? Or something more?

With sticky notes and hints galore,
Ambivalence knocks at my core.
Should I choose this? Or that instead?
A chicken dance or 'go to bed'?

Friends say, "Flip a coin," they cheer,
But does it ever bring me near?
Answers hide, oh what a tease,
While I'm lost in this quirky breeze.

In the maze, I pirouette,
Finding laughter, no regret.
With jumbled thoughts, I shout, "Let's play!"
And wander off, come what may.

Seeking Straight Answers

In a game of verbal ping-pong,
I plead for truth, it feels so wrong.
Why the mystery? What's the fuss?
Life's a riddle, no need to rush!

Why is bread round, but toast square?
Do questions float on goofy air?
With every quip, I seek the clue,
Munching on thoughts, like morning dew.

Right or left? Just make a call,
If you could only shed some light, at all.
Do birds know where the worms reside?
Or do they just find joy in the glide?

So here I sit, a little bemused,
As the world spins, slightly confused.
With a grin, I'll take my chance,
At the chaos, I'll laugh and dance.

The Halting Progress of Understanding

In a maze of facts, I twist and turn,
Each path a lesson, but still I yearn.
Like a gopher in a hole, I dig and dive,
Seeking the nugget that might help me thrive.

With charts and graphs, I start to plot,
But halfway through, I've forgotten the thought.
A light bulb flickers, then blinks out fast,
I'm just a shadow of all I've amassed.

I raise my hand, the teacher sighs,
As I ask a question that's full of "whys."
They nod and smile, but I still feel lost,
The price of knowledge, an unpredictable cost.

So here I stand, with scribbles and scrawls,
Chasing the answers through endless halls.
Maybe one day, I'll break this spell,
For now, it's a circus where I know too well.

Insights Just Out of Reach

I chase bright ideas like a cat with a string,
Every small flicker makes my hope take wing.
Yet when I grab, it vanishes fast,
A cruel little trick that leaves me aghast.

Like catching smoke, I stretch out my hand,
But insights slip through, so cunningly planned.
I ponder and frown, the clock counts down,
Turning to humor to drown out the frown.

I scribble a note then lose my own thread,
Thus creating confusion with each word said.
It's comedy gold, though I play the fool,
In a dance with clarity, where none are the rules.

So here's to the musings that tease and evade,
I'll laugh all the way through this grand charade.
The truth waits somewhere, behind a great wall,
I'll trip on my shoelaces, but I'll still stand tall.

Searching for the Tailwind

With dreams on my back, I set off today,
To find that elusive, swift tailwind play.
But every gust seems to blow the wrong way,
Am I just a kite in a grand disarray?

In books of wisdom, I search for clues,
Only to find I'm wearing the wrong shoes.
Page after page, the wisdom eludes,
As my queries dance like rambunctious dudes.

I climb to the peak, but wait, what's this?
A view so confusing, it feels like a quiz!
I laugh at the struggle, for laughter is free,
As I whirl with the wind, a leaf from a tree.

So off I roam, with thoughts in the air,
Chasing the whispers that go with a glare.
Maybe someday, I'll sail with that breeze,
Till then, I'm content with my playful unease.

The Elusive Grapes of Clarity

I reach for the grapes that hang just up high,
They shimmer with knowledge, as dreams pass by.
But each time I stretch, they bob and they sway,
I'm left with my fingers, unable to play.

In the garden of logic, I tend with care,
Searching for answers that dance in thin air.
Hints bloom like flowers, but petals fall away,
Leaving me puzzled through another lost day.

I ponder in circles, I scribble and fuss,
About the nature of answers, oh what a plus!
Yet laughter erupts as I trip on my wit,
In this uphill climb, isn't laughter a hit?

So I pluck at the thought, as the season fades,
Turning confusion into sweet escapades.
In this chase for the grapes, I'll find some delight,
With a smile and a wink, and a twinkle of light.

The Unraveled Thread

In a world of tangled thoughts,
I search for clarity, it's fraught.
An endless game of hide and seek,
The answers wave and never speak.

A friend once promised he'd explain,
His words just added to my brain strain.
I asked for light; he brought a joke,
Now I'm lost in the punchline's smoke.

Navigating life like a GPS fails,
Recalculating through endless details.
Instructions scribbled on a napkin,
But all it says is: "Hurry and fasten!"

Oh wisdom, where's your clever guide?
On this crazy rollercoaster ride.
If knowledge is power, I'm feeling weak,
Just give me a clue, or a funny leak!

Moments of Frustration

I sat at a table, coffee in hand,
Trying to figure out life's grand plan.
The barista smiled, but she just brewed,
Nothing of sense, just thick mist of food.

An old man whispered a wise old tale,
Only to lose me with his own detail.
A riddle so complex, it left me perplexed,
To uncover the truth, I'll need a crude text.

My cat, the guru, sleeps on the sill,
While I ponder over life's uphill thrill.
Perhaps the meaning's in the purrs,
Or tangled in yarn, or lost in slurs.

So onwards I chase the elusive light,
Through humorous trials, a curious plight.
I'm stumped but smiling, chasing my fate,
Perhaps this mystery is best left to fate!

The Dance of Doubt

A waltz in my mind, thoughts twisting and twirling,
Around and around, my worries keep swirling.
Doubt does the tango, insistently bold,
While reason just sits, feeling a bit cold.

I asked my reflection, "What's the next move?"
It shrugged its shoulders, it seemed to disprove.
Each step feels haunted by questions unreal,
Yet they waltz in my head, an absurd reel.

The clock has its own beat, ticking in sync,
But wait… was that right, or am I on the brink?
Every answer feels like a misstep tonight,
As I trip over laughter in the pale light.

With every stumble, I giggle and sigh,
Who knew life's dance would leave me awry?
I'll keep on spinning through chaos and cheer,
Embracing the laughter, where questions appear!

In the Fog of Unknowns

A fog rolls in, thick and real,
It whispers secrets I can't quite feel.
Each step I take is uncertain, vague,
Like solving a puzzle with pieces that plague.

I asked the clouds, "What's the deal up there?"
They laughed and floated, without a care.
An answer elusive, it echoed in jest,
"Finding the point? That's quite a quest!"

My thoughts drifted like leaves on a stream,
Searching for clarity, chasing a dream.
Yet here comes the punchline, a twist of fate,
Maybe confusion's just love that waits.

I'll wander this fog with a laugh and a grin,
In the mystery lies the fun to begin.
The journey's the jest, while the questions parade,
And joy finds its way through the playful charade.

The Labyrinth of Logic

In a maze of thoughts I find,
Twists and turns, so unkind.
With every step, a question grows,
Yet the answer always goes.

Purpose hides in jumbled words,
Like a flock of confused birds.
I chase shadows in my mind,
While clarity is left behind.

Puzzles piled in rhyme and jest,
Each one trying to outsmart the rest.
If I only had a map,
To avoid this mental trap!

So grab a snack, and take a seat,
As fun's the only thing I meet.
In circles round we dance and prance,
For logic leads a silly dance.

Questions Dressed in Circles

Round and round the questions spin,
Dressed in riddles, where to begin?
They wear their gowns of mystery,
While I sip tea in history.

What's the point? Ah yes, the crux,
But all I hear are random flux.
Like socks that vanish in the wash,
Answers dart, then take a nosh.

They prance about in fancy suits,
Pretending they've got solid roots.
When all I want is a straight line,
And not this fuss that feels like wine.

Yet here I am, still sipping slow,
As circular thoughts continue to flow.
Perhaps the game is just for fun,
To laugh until the day is done.

The Heart of the Matter

At the core, what is the deal?
I dig and dig, but can't feel real.
Love, logic, or just pure haze?
I'm caught in an endless maze.

Tell me quick, don't string me out,
I'm hungry for clarity, no doubt.
Yet all I hear are silly quips,
That dance around like eager lips.

The heart beats loud, but what's the beat?
Like a child lost at a candy treat.
I ponder deep in this messy jam,
Is it logic, or just wham-bam?

With every twist, a chuckle bursts,
Like chocolate flowing from sweet quirks.
So let's have fun in this wild plot,
Who needs the heart? Just give me what's hot!

Unraveled Mysteries

The night is young, questions unfold,
Wrapped in tales that can't be told.
Like socks that hide in time's embrace,
I search for sense in every space.

Whispers tease with silver words,
Yet I'm trapped like lonely birds.
The clock ticks on, still no release,
As I beg for sweet, sweet peace.

What's the secret in this jest?
A treasure map or a fuzzy quest?
I'd settle for an evening snack,
If only logic would come back.

So here I sit, in laughter's thrall,
As nonsense reigns, despite it all.
Life's rich tapestry, tangled and wry,
With every thread, I chuckle and sigh.

Unpacking the Mystery

I unwrap my thoughts so slow,
Like tangled lights from long ago.
What's the reason, what's the plan?
Inside my head, a buzzing fan.

With every clue, a twist I find,
A cat with secrets on its mind.
Answers dance just out of reach,
While I'm left to ponder, preach.

Maps and charts I lay in vain,
All these symbols drive me insane.
Like hiding gifts underneath the bed,
I'm left with nonsense in my head.

So here I sit, a curious one,
Trying to decipher just for fun.
Is there logic? Can it be?
Or just a chuckle meant for me?

Threads of Truth

Life's a loom with colors bright,
Weave the fabric of delight.
Yet each thread pulls at my mind,
What's the purpose? Is there, kind?

Questions hang like laundry tossed,
In the breeze, my clarity lost.
Knots of meaning tight and bold,
But it's just yarn, or so I'm told.

Tug and yank, unravel slow,
The answers hide, they do not show.
Jokes on me, or am I jest?
This riddle game's a wild quest.

With every stitch, a chuckle grows,
In this tangle, more humor shows.
Maybe it's all just a fun spree,
A cosmic joke played on me!

What Lies Beneath the Riddles?

Wrapped in riddles, tight and neat,
Like a puzzle hiding in sweet.
I chase the shadows, what's the deal?
A hidden truth, or just a meal?

Words like feathers float around,
Whispers echo, hollow sound.
Are they secrets or a game?
More like a dog with no real name.

I flip the pages, seek the clue,
But each answer sounds like stew.
A metaphorical soup I sip,
Missing the boat, I start to trip.

Oh laughter thrives in cryptic thoughts,
As I juggle all I've sought.
Perhaps the point skips all around,
A prankster's laugh is what I found!

The Weight of Unsaid Words

Heavy thoughts, a mountain high,
Words unspoken, oh my, oh my!
Like a suitcase packed with doubt,
I haul it round, what's it about?

Tick-tock, my mind's a clock,
Yet every second feels like a rock.
What if silence speaks the loudest?
In whispered truths, I'm the proudest.

Weighty sighs collect like dust,
What's this meaning I must trust?
Crumpled notes in pockets lie,
Hints of words I still must try.

So I laugh and shuffle through,
This comic dance I'm forced to do.
Perhaps in jest, I'll find the thread,
For silly things my heart has said.

The Labyrinth of Insight

I wandered through this maze of words,
Hoping for a clue or two,
Questions circling, minds absurd,
Where's the exit? Tell me who.

Spinning tales with baffled glee,
Lost in riddles, such a feat!
Just a hint, oh won't you see?
I trip on logic's dancing feet.

Echoes of wisdom tease and taunt,
Like cats playing with a string,
I asked the sage, he said, "You want?"
"How much for the real thing?"

Endlessly I quest for sense,
But clarity hides its clever face,
In this maze of suspense,
I need a guide to quicken the pace.

Craving Straight Talk

With every subtle hint I yearn,
For a voice that speaks in plain,
Words so structured, crisp, and firm,
Not wrapped in jargon's sweet disdain.

I sift through layers deep and wide,
With metaphors that twist and spin,
Where's the truth? I need a guide,
To cut the fluff and let me in!

Conversations like a buffet,
I'm starving for the naked truth,
But all I get is gourmet play,
"Guess what?" they say, like it's some sleuth!

Let's drop the games, I plead with glee,
Reveal the essence, strip it bare,
I crave the point and its decree,
No sugarcoating, just lay it there.

Where is the Compass?

In the forest of uncertainty,
I lost my way and stolen shoes,
Thoughts like leaves dance free and wild,
Yet clarity remains so far to choose.

I asked a bird to show the way,
Instead, it sang a cryptic song,
"Chirp, chirp!" it said, "Come what may,"
I wondered if I was doing wrong.

Cloudy skies and fog so thick,
This map I hold is full of woe,
"Find the point!" the compass pricks,
But it spins round, and round, and slow.

Where's the North when I need a break?
Reality hides behind a grin,
Finding truth is no small stake,
Just point me right, and let me win!

Chasing Shadows of Understanding

In a dance with shadows I now dwell,
They flicker, teasing with a sway,
I chase the whispers, hear them tell,
What's clear today might fade away.

Asking questions like they're snacks,
Hungry for knowledge but getting crumbs,
I dive into conversational hacks,
But all I gather is mental hums.

Like a joke without the punchline set,
These shadows laugh, and I just frown,
Dodging answers, we're stuck in debt,
When will this merry-go-round slow down?

So I'll keep running, chasing light,
Until I catch that glimmer bright,
For in the end, it feels so right,
To find the truth, say, "That's the sight!"

In Search of a Straight Answer

Why does every answer twist and turn,
Like a long-winded lecture we didn't earn?
I ask 'What's the time?' and get a whole tale,
About the sun and the moon, and it starts to sail.

Clocks seem to giggle, they tick and they tock,
While I stand here confused, searching for the clock.
Can't someone just hand me a simple reply?
Instead of a story that makes me want to cry!

I nod and I smile, trying to engage,
As answers are hidden behind a grand stage.
But when I seek clarity, I'm met with a jest,
A riddle's more straight than this humorous quest.

So here's to the talks with no end in sight,
Where I'm left in a quandary, lost in the light.
Next time, dear friend, just give me the scoop,
Or I might just stroll off and join a cat troop!

The Weight of Unfinished Thoughts

I ponder and I muse, what was that they said?
Answers float around like balloons in my head.
Each thought unfinished dangles in the air,
Like socks on a line, unwashed and laid bare.

The sage on the corner, with wisdom to share,
Spins yarns of the cosmos and life's endless dare.
I came for the wisdom, not folklore or myth,
But I'm trapped in their stories; oh, how do I sift?

I chuckle and grin, as they pull at my string,
With conclusions unclear, like a dog chasing bling.
I wait for that moment, the piece that will fit,
Yet I'm still here chuckling, just stuck in their wit.

Oh, what can a mind do with thoughts weighty and free?
I'm lost in the jokes, where's the clarity?
If you've got the answer, throw me a bone,
Or leave me to wander this perplexing zone!

Decoding the Unsaid

In a world full of whispers, where meanings get blurred,
I look for the logic in what's never heard.
The signs and the winks, like a secretive dance,
Leave me more puzzled, caught up in a trance.

Conversations like puzzles with pieces all jumbled,
The messages tangled, my poor brain is crumbled.
I nod in agreement, pretending I know,
But I'm diving in deep, where the currents don't flow.

I raise up my hand, like a kid wanting in,
But the clues remain closed, locked up in a grin.
I sigh and I laugh at this curious game,
As meanings elude me, like wind and a flame.

So here's to the chats that lead us astray,
Where those unspoken thoughts find their playful sway.
If you've got the key to this riddle's delight,
Just slip it my way in the still of the night!

Waiting for the Aha Moment

I sit on the edge, waiting, all ears,
For a brilliant insight to calm all my fears.
Yet the clock just keeps ticking, seconds unfold,
While laughter and riddles endlessly scold.

They talk and they chuckle, with wisdom they weave,
But answers are cloaked, like tricks up their sleeve.
I lean in so close, hoping for that spark,
But humor's the boss, drowning out my remark.

So pass me the popcorn, I'll watch from my seat,
As minds play their games, my patience is beat.
I'm pondering hard, where's that moment of truth?
But the giggles keep rolling, oh youth is uncouth.

I search for the punchline, the grand revelation,
But all I find here is fun and frustration.
If the answer should come, let it drop like a stone,
Till then I'll just sit here, and chuckle alone!

The Art of Knowing

Why is the sky blue? They shrug with a grin,
The answer slips away, just like the wind.
A rabbit in the hat but where's the trick?
Searching for answers, it's making me sick.

I ask a philosopher, he ponders too long,
Sipping his tea, he hums a soft song.
"Life's a puzzle," he smirks with delight,
But I just want clarity, not philosophical fright.

The wise say they know, but do they really?
I smile politely and feel a bit silly.
They laugh at my quest, as I scratch my head,
For wisdom's a noodle that's hard to be fed.

So here's to the jesters, the jesters of truth,
Whose riddles and rhymes dance around like youth.
In this grand circus, forget about the score,
The point is the journey, and maybe there's more.

Beneath the Surface

What's with the fish? They swim up and down,
Does anyone know why they wear that frown?
They flip and they flop, no map in their fins,
Just swimming in circles, like life's little sins.

I ponder the ocean, so vast and so blue,
"Do you have a plan?" I whisper to a whale too.
She rolls her big eyes, says, "I just float by,
Beneath the surface, where the crazy fish lie."

The coral looks puzzled, with colors so bright,
They sparkle and shine, but what's their insight?
As the currents tease tales of deep-sea delight,
The point of it all seems to drift out of sight.

I lean on a rock, feeling slightly absurd,
Grinning at fish tales, awaiting a word.
But silence from depths is quite common I find,
Perhaps the ocean's just teasing my mind.

In Quest of Purpose

Off on the quest, with my map and my snack,
Searching for something; I don't know what's lack.
Each twist and each turn, I'm keen to explore,
But where is the treasure? Oh, what's it for?

The wise man I meet is busy with rocks,
Duct-taping fate into mismatched socks.
He chuckles and says, "It's all in your head,
Perhaps your true purpose is right in your bed."

I ponder the words, yes, while snuggled in sheets,
Is the meaning of life just some cozy retreats?
My dreams filled with donuts and magical quests,
Maybe the point is to simply be blessed.

So I grab my remote, cozied up for a show,
With each laugh and each story, I'm starting to know.
The quest for a purpose is sometimes a jest,
Embrace the absurd – it's not such a test!

The Void of Ambiguity

In a world of fog, where clarity shies,
Words swirl like leaves under dark, cloudy skies.
I ask for a sign, maybe two or three more,
But the answers are cryptic; I'm left at the door.

Ambiguity greets me with a mischievous wink,
Like a cat on a fence, it just loves to think.
"What's up with the math?" I query the stars,
They dance and they twinkle, but leave lots of scars.

The meaning of life is a grand game of charades,
Filled with laughter, confusion, and soft serenades.
I try to decode it with giggles and sighs,
But all I can muster are half-hearted tries.

So let's raise a glass to the vague and the strange,
For mystery's charm is a welcome exchange.
In this crazy old riddle, so messy and vast,
The point isn't the answer; it's just having a blast.

Where to from Here?

I woke up today, what's next on the list?
With coffee in hand, I shouldn't exist.
Plans scribbled in haste, a scribble for sure,
But what's the big prize, or is there a cure?

Like a map in my pocket, directions I lack,
I thought I was clever, now I'm under attack.
Oh, where do I wander, oh what will I find?
A sign that says 'Go!' or a warning from mankind?

In moments of chaos, the clock starts to spin,
Do I chase after trends, or just stick to my kin?
With questions aplenty and answers so few,
I giggle at fate while I sip my cold brew.

Perhaps there's a treasure, or just a long ride,
The journey to nowhere, so let's enjoy the glide.
Amusement in wandering, a laugh in the cheer,
So here's to the mystery, let's toast with a beer!

The Lingering Question

What's cooking today, is it soup or a stew?
Or maybe a mystery with a pinch of déjà vu?
I glance at the menu, my choice seems so bleak,
But surely there's wisdom, if only you'd speak!

The waiter just smiles, a grin ear to ear,
Dish of the day, yet it still isn't clear.
"Do you recommend it?" I ask, a bit glum,
His nod is so vague, I just want to run.

Should I take the leap, or stick with the safe?
The process of choosing, oh what a mad chase!
Do I want the thrill or the comfort of bread?
Each dish is a puzzle, but who'll solve instead?

In circles we spiral, the dining room laughs,
Indecision at play, like we're painting with halves.
So here in this diner, I ponder my quest,
For answers elusive, I'll just take a rest!

The Quest for the Essential

I hunt for the secret, the gem in the rough,
The meaning of life, is it ever enough?
With maps made of riddles, I can't find my way,
It's like searching for socks that just vanish in gray.

People with answers, they talk all around,
With big grand ideas that are oddly profound.
But really, dear friend, can't we just have fun?
Keep it light and breezy, or are we all done?

The quest for essentials turns into a game,
With players confused, yet all shout with the same:
"What's life if it lacks a good joke or a laugh?"
So I'll take silly moments, and just do the math.

Perhaps in the chaos, the point's simply this,
Life's not just a stairway, it's a dance, it's a kiss.
So I'll skip the deep answers and enjoy the parade,
In the laughter of friends, I'll find what I've made!

Conversations in Circles

We gather in circles, with coffee in hand,
Discussing the cosmos, as if we had a plan.
Topics like weather or who's winning the game,
Yet we don't touch the surface, it's all just the same.

What's that in the corner? A question so bold,
But like playful cats, it's a dance to behold.
We pounce on each thought, but they slip through our grip,
Debates go in spirals, it's a wobbly trip.

To ponder or wander, what's real and what's fake?
Like chasing a shadow, and we're losing the stake.
Somehow it feels nice, despite all our squabbles,
With laughter and coffee, we laugh through our troubles.

So here's to the chatter, the talk that we share,
In circles we giggle, in mismatched foot wear.
The point isn't pointed; it's a big lack of risk,
But honestly, dear friends, aren't we all just a whisk?

The Essence Eludes

In circles we run, with puzzled frowns,
Chasing the facts, they keep slipping down.
With quirky gestures and raised eyebrows,
We dig for the gold, but we only find crows.

A philosopher's jest, we ponder and rave,
The meaning of meaning, we just cannot save.
Our glasses are empty, yet we keep on sipping,
In a quest for the truth, but the truth is still tripping.

Unraveled Questions

Why's the sky blue? Is that really a thing?
When time flies a kite, does it always sing?
With loops in our thoughts, we tap our chins tight,
We chase after insights that dance out of sight.

A riddle in riddles, with twists that amaze,
We laugh through the chaos, lost in a haze.
Thinking of answers, like the cat in the hat,
Should we flip it for fun, or just leave it at that?

Whispers of Clarity

In the shadows of mind, where doubts play and tease,
Whispers of clarity tease like the breeze.
We ponder like owls, with wisdom so sly,
Yet answers come wrapped in a riddle-y sigh.

A squirrel in a tree, with a nut on its head,
In a race for the prize, we just end up misled.
With giggles and snorts, we twist and we turn,
In search of the wisdom, for which we must yearn.

Maps to Nowhere

With each marked step, we veer off the trail,
Maps to nowhere; we giggle and flail.
Compass spinning wildly, emotions on high,
Who needs a destination? Just let's fly high!

Like sheep with a plan, we wander and roam,
When the map leads to ice cream, we feel right at home.
In laughter we find that it's not about haste,
But the joy in the journey and the friends that we chase.

What Are We Waiting For?

Tick tock goes the clock,
Coffee's gone cold, what a shock.
Time's a riddle, wrapped in fluff,
Why's it gotta be so tough?

Got plans written in the stars,
But all I see are rusty cars.
Let's skip the talks of fate,
And just order up some cake!

Each change of season, same old game,
I swear it's all just a big name.
With lost time and gained regret,
Let's have fun 'til we forget!

So raise your glass, let's have a cheer,
For questions we might never clear.
The point's elusive, that's the jest,
But laughter, my friend, is the best.

The Landscape of Longing

In fields where dreams do twirl around,
Why do we always look for ground?
Hills of fortune, valleys of doubt,
Maybe it's time to just shout!

Painted skies, a canvas wide,
Why not take a crazy ride?
Chasing shadows with a grin,
Who knows what's just 'round the bin?

Thoughts like clouds up in the blue,
What's the fuss? I haven't a clue.
Instead of seeking grand designs,
Let's have ice cream and share some lines!

Longing's a game, let's play it well,
Turn the absurd into a spell.
When questions dance on fingertips,
Let's write our own amusing scripts!

A Tangled Web of Thoughts

In corners of my busy mind,
I search for clarity, but I find,
A web of thoughts that twist and spin,
What's the prize for this big win?

Do I ponder, fret, and sigh?
Or launch my hopes into the sky?
The answers hide, they pull the shroud,
So let's take selfies—say it loud!

Caught in nets of playful jest,
Tangled tales put to the test.
Who needs the reason, who needs the rhyme?
Let's dance like it's the end of time!

Questions dangle like the stars,
What's the catch behind the bars?
So let's toast to unknown roads,
And laugh off all these heavy loads.

Hints of Hidden Truth

Behind each smile, a secret lies,
In puzzled faces, truth complies.
Signs of laughter, winks of fate,
Why is it all so hard to rate?

Like trying to fit a square in round,
I search for gems that won't be found.
Between the lines of every phrase,
Wait—did I just lose my gaze?

Whispers float like candy floss,
But what's the point if we're at a loss?
Let's turn this chase into a play,
Where riddles dance and flip away!

Truth's a riddle that makes us grin,
So let's wear our questions like a pin.
In laughter's arms, let's find the clue,
The path to fun is always new!

Epiphanies at Dusk

As daylight fades, ideas collide,
Thoughts like fireflies in the night.
What's the answer? I've lost my guide,
Just a twist of fate feels so right.

I ponder life's riddles, all tangled tight,
With every sip of my too-cold drink.
Is there wisdom in this silly plight?
Or is it all just in how we think?

Fumbling through laughs and shady chats,
The punchline's near, I can feel it come.
But all I find are these silly spats,
Life's a game, but where's the fun?

Fleeting moments, like bubbles that burst,
Each one a whisper, a ticklish tease.
I search for clarity, but it's still cursed,
Keeping me laughing, a life just to please.

The Question Hangs Heavy

A question floats like unkempt hair,
Tugging on thoughts with no clear lead.
Why chase answers like they're in the air?
The cliff of confusion plants a seed.

Jokes tumble out in a messy rant,
Searching for logic in a quirky play.
Each punchline stings like a raging chant,
Yet here I am, still lost in the fray.

Laughter echoes through the crowded space,
As we twirl around, a dizzying jest.
Each inquiry pulls with a scowling face,
Why is the query a forever quest?

As smiles flicker in the midst of doubt,
We ponder questions that won't unfold.
In funny chaos, we twist and shout,
Perhaps the answers are just too bold!

Spectrum of Meaning

In a colorful world of varied hues,
Where meanings shift with each little blink.
I chase the rainbow, a playful muse,
As logic slips through like sand in a sink.

Why does humor dance in wavy lines?
A riddle wrapped in a joke all alone.
With every laugh, the tension unwinds,
Yet still I wonder if I am home.

Clouds of intellect drift far and wide,
Yet clarity plays hide and seek with fate.
Every chuckle is a playful guide,
But understanding? Now that can wait!

At the crossroads of giggles and sighs,
I find it funny how answers love to flee.
In this silly search for the wisest prize,
The journey's the punchline, not just a decree.

The Quest for Certainty

On my quest for wisdom, I twirl and spin,
With questions dangling like signs in the breeze.
Is finding answers just a game to win,
Or a folly washed up like driftwood seas?

Each inquiry's a feather, light as air,
Drifting away on a laugh-filled tide.
While truth darts around, oh, how it dares,
A playful cat that won't let me inside.

I leap through puns, stumbling over my feet,
As solid ground shifts like a dance on sand.
With each chuckle, I feel life's heartbeat,
Yet clarity hides, lending a helping hand.

In the end, it's a glorious jest,
With every question, a giggle unfurls.
Perhaps the point's lost in this confounding fest,
And laughter, dear friend, is the gem of the world.

www.ingramcontent.com/pod-product-compliance
Lightning Source LLC
Chambersburg PA
CBHW051654160426
43209CB00004B/893